Yay!
You Failed!

Shannon Anderson

Illustrated by Steve Mark

free spirit
PUBLISHING®

Text copyright © 2022 Shannon Anderson
Illustrations copyright © 2022 Free Spirit Publishing

Library of Congress Cataloging-in-Publication Data
Names: Anderson, Shannon, 1972– author. | Mark, Steve, illustrator.
Title: Yay! You failed! / by Shannon Anderson ; illustrated by Steve Mark.
Description: Minneapolis, MN : Free Spirit Publishing Inc., [2022] | Series: Little laugh & learn | Audience: Ages 6–9
Identifiers: LCCN 2021060479 (print) | LCCN 2021060480 (ebook) | ISBN 9781631987199 (paperback) | ISBN 9781631987205 (pdf) | ISBN 9781631987212 (epub)
Subjects: LCSH: Attitude (Psychology)—Juvenile literature. | Achievement motivation in children—Juvenile literature.
Classification: LCC BF327 .A536 2022 (print) | LCC BF327 (ebook) | DDC 155.4/18232—dc23/eng/20220127
LC record available at https://lccn.loc.gov/2021060479
LC ebook record available at https://lccn.loc.gov/2021060480

Edited by Eric Braun
Cover and interior design by Emily Dyer

Printed in China

Free Spirit Publishing
An imprint of Teacher Created Materials
6325 Sandburg Road, Suite 100
Minneapolis, MN 55427-3674
(612) 338-2068
help4kids@freespirit.com
freespirit.com

FSC
www.fsc.org
MIX
Paper from
responsible sources
FSC® C144853

Dedication

This book is dedicated to all the kids who believe in the power of learning from our mistakes.

Acknowledgments

I want to acknowledge my editor, Eric Braun, who is an encourager and who provides positive feedback to help me grow!

CONTENTS

CHAPTER 1

What You Can Do When You Believe in You

Do you have a "Can Do" attitude?
When you want to try something new,
do you believe you CAN DO it? When
you want to get better at something,
do you think . . .

That's something I CAN DO!

1

The Power of a Growth Mindset

Your attitude toward trying things is called your **mindset**. When you believe you can learn and get better at something, you have a growth mindset. Maybe you're trying to learn to

- ride a bike

- create a diorama

- train your dog

- bake cookies

- finish a puzzle

- draw dinosaurs

- tie your shoes

Having a growth mindset is like having superpowers. Believing is the first step toward taking action. You are telling your brain to go for it. You give yourself the chance to do new things. You can become a new, SUPER version of yourself.

I can scare away every squirrel!

I set goals!

I keep practicing!

I try new things!

I learn from my mistakes!

I don't give up!

I have a good attitude!

5

Don't Get Fixed in One Place

The opposite of a growth mindset is a **fixed mindset**. People who have a fixed mindset about something *don't* believe they are able to learn it.

When you don't believe in yourself, it's easy to give up. If you give up, you can't succeed.

Someone with a fixed mindset might say . . .

I can't do it.

It's too hard.

I'm just not a math person.

When you have thoughts like that, it's harder to believe in yourself. You are less likely to try. You tell your brain not to go for it.

Why might someone feel this way?
Maybe they are worried they can't do it.
Maybe they worry someone will laugh
at them. Because of their worries, they
decide not to give it a try.

Here's a little secret: You should give
it a try anyway. Keep reading and you'll
see why.

CHAPTER 2

Practice Makes Progress

Is anything in life perfect? The perfect s'more! The perfect summer day! Those might be pretty darn great. Maybe even close to perfect. But can *people* be perfect?

Maybe you've heard someone say, "Practice makes perfect." It's a nice idea, but it's not quite right. The truth is that practice makes **progress**.

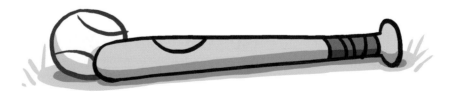

Think about batting. No matter how much you practice, you will never be "perfect" at hitting the ball. You can get much better. You can hit it more often and strike out less. But you won't hit it every single time. Not even the biggest pro superstars can do that.

Getting Better, Stitch by Stitch

Imagine you see someone do something really cool, like sew a stuffed animal. They surely had to practice sewing simpler pieces first.

Maybe it went like this: They learned how to thread a needle and knot the thread. Then they practiced stitching a straight line.

Next, they learned how to make a
square pillow. After that, they learned
how to use a pattern.

After all of that, they felt ready to
make a stuffed animal, with some help.

Everyone starts out as a beginner. Your dad may be great at baking cookies now. But the first time he made them, he may not have done a good job measuring ingredients. Or he may have burned a batch or two. He learned and got better.

It is normal to need to practice a task many times. When we keep at it, we get better. It gets a little easier. This applies to playing the piano and learning to paint. It's the same for learning your math facts, learning a new sport, and any other new things you try.

Make Progress with the Success Cycle

As you work on a new skill, think about going through the Success Cycle.

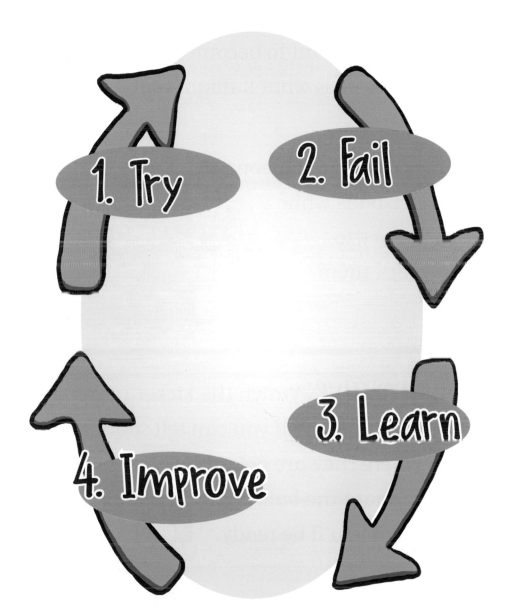

Let's take the example of soccer. Maybe you want to become a better goalie. Here is what it might look like:

1. **Try:** Have someone kick balls while you try to block them.

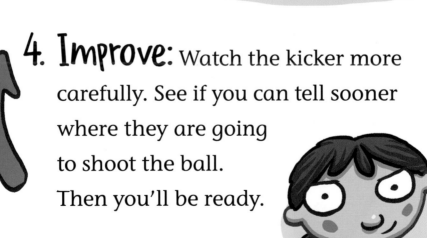

4. **Improve:** Watch the kicker more carefully. See if you can tell sooner where they are going to shoot the ball. Then you'll be ready.

2. Fail: A lot of balls get past you.

3. Learn: You need to be quicker on shots in the corners.

When you fail, the Success Cycle always leads you back to **Step 1: Try**. As you repeat the Success Cycle, you keep getting better at what you're doing. That means you are making progress. You just haven't mastered it *yet*.

Yet is a powerful word. It's a word of hope. It means you believe in yourself. You believe that with enough practice, you can eventually meet your goal.

If you ever hear someone say, "I can't do this," you can be an encouraging friend. Say, "No, you just haven't gotten it *yet*. You'll get it if you keep practicing."

24

Success Cycle Tip

Be careful not to skip the "Learn" part of the cycle. If you just keep doing the Try and Fail steps without the Learn step, you will never get to the Improve part.

Pay attention to what went right and what went wrong. Maybe you have good aim with your free throw but it keeps bouncing off the rim. You might need to arc the ball higher. Or maybe you're trying to memorize a song and you keep messing up the same line. You might need to study that line a little extra.

The more you practice, the more progress you will make. Pretty soon the Success Cycle will lead to . . .

. . . you guessed it . . .

Success!

Three Ways to Keep Going When the Going Gets Tough

It happens to everyone. There will be times you are working on something and it gets hard. Like, *really* hard. Maybe you're trying to do a cartwheel, and you

30

keep falling over. Maybe you've tried the Success Cycle over and over and over. Maybe you've tried so many times you want to quit. You feel like it will never be easy for you.

Sometimes when we fail, it can be hard to keep going. But you can learn how to *bounce back* from a *setback* and give it another try. That's called being **resilient**.

Resilient isn't easy to say, and it isn't an easy thing to be sometimes. Here are three tips to help you find that CAN DO attitude.

Tip #1: Take a Break

When you start to feel frustrated, it can help to give yourself a little break. Stop doing what you're doing for a while. Maybe you're playing chess or learning to ride a bike. Maybe you're trying to get better at swimming. Maybe you're training your dog. Whatever it is, step away from it and start fresh tomorrow. You may be less tired and more focused. You may have had time to think about new ways to try again.

Tip #2:
Use Positive Self-Talk

Sometimes being resilient means being your own cheerleader. Encourage yourself with positive messages. You can say . . .

"I can do hard things!"

"The struggle makes me stronger!"

"I'm proud of myself for trying!"

You can say these messages out loud or just inside your head. You can even make mini-posters with quotes or sticky notes that help you remember your growth mindset thinking. You know what's fun? Find a friend who will hoot and holler for you.

Master those spelling words.

Keep on trying

I can get better

Tip #3: Get Help

One thing that is SUPER helpful is having someone with more experience coach you. Is there someone you trust who is good at the thing you are trying? It could be a teacher, coach, mentor, family member, or friend. They can give you **feedback**. That means they watch you work and give you advice on how to get better. Listening to their advice is a great way to improve.

CHAPTER 4

Ready . . . Set . . . Goal!

Sometimes you want to learn something that is easy-peasy-lemon-squeezy. It might not take much work to figure out. But sometimes what you want to learn is harder.

It might be playing the piano or counting to 100 in a new (to you!) language. It might be mastering a fancy card trick. Stuff like that takes more work. It can help to set a **goal.**

AWESOME CARD tricks

Let's say you want to draw your dog. You give it a try, but it turns out more like a hairy crocodile. You could set a goal to learn how to draw your dog so it looks like a dog.

What would you like to learn or challenge yourself to try?

- Is there a sport or game you'd like to learn to play or get better at?

- Is there a craft, like origami, that you'd like to figure out?

- Do you want to read a certain number of books in the next month?

Three Steps for Setting and Reaching a Goal

Step 1: **Write it down.** You could write your goal on a sticky note and put it somewhere you will see it each day as a reminder. Or write it in a notebook. Seeing the goal every day will help you stay focused on it.

Step 2: Think about *how* you can do it. Do you just need to practice? Would it help to join a club or team to learn skills? Or take a class? Maybe you can learn from an online video. Or maybe someone you know can teach you.

Step 3: Give yourself an end date.

When do you want to finish learning this new skill? Having an end date or deadline can help keep you focused.

Choose an end date that is realistic but challenging. Don't make it so far in the future that you forget about it. But don't make it so soon that it will be impossible to meet. You can ask an adult to help you figure out a good deadline.

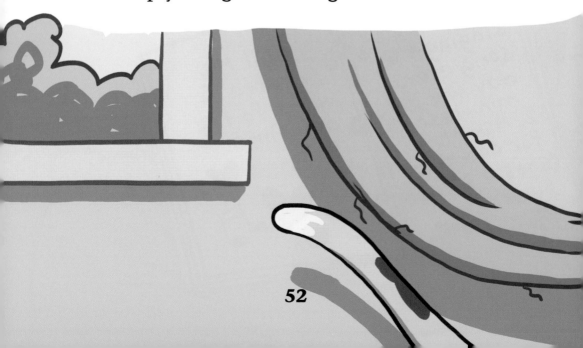

53

Bonus Step: Break It Down

Are you trying to do something really big and hard? It can help to break big goals down into smaller parts. Maybe even teeny-tiny parts. These smaller goals can help you see your progress.

Clean Your Room

Day 1: Put away underwear.

-Put dishes in sink.

-Vacuum rug.

It can be hard to be patient while you are learning the sign language alphabet. Try breaking the goal down into learning one letter per day. One letter a day isn't so hard! That takes the pressure off.

Make sure your smaller goals work with your deadline. If you're learning the sign language alphabet, make your deadline 26 days away. That's one day for each letter. Again, an adult can help you with this.

A Look on the Bright Side

The road to growth can sometimes be tricky and hard. It might be tough to stay positive. But you can learn to look on the bright side. That helps you keep trying. Here are a few tips.

Take Time to Celebrate

You don't have to wait until you have met your goal to feel good about it. You can always feel good about your efforts. You can even celebrate when you come up short. It means you are still trying. Sticking with it is worth celebrating.

Each step in the right direction deserves a high five!

61

Picture Success

Let's say you get a lot wrong on a quiz or mess up at your piano recital. Maybe you skin your knee learning a trick on your skateboard. How can you find the bright side of these moments?

Think of how good it will feel when you finally do succeed. Picture yourself winning the game. See yourself playing that song well or mastering that skateboard trick. That peek at success can keep you feeling positive. It may motivate you to work harder.

Turn Around the What-If Monster

Have you ever had the "What-If Monster" in your head? You know, the voice that says things like:

- What if you fail?

- What if they laugh at you?

- What if you never figure it out?

You can flip those statements around:

- What if I do better than I did last time?
- What if they cheer for me?
- What if I *do* figure it out?

No Fair to Compare

Looking on the bright side means you don't compare yourself to someone else. Don't worry about the progress of others. What's important is that you do better than YOU have done in the past.

Think about making popcorn. The kernels are all cooked together at the same temperature. They cook for the same amount of time. But they don't all pop at the same time. Nope! First you hear a few pop, then a few more. Then you hear a bunch more pop. Finally the last few go pop, pop, pop . . .

. . . pop!

People are like those kernels. You can be in the same classroom with the same teacher. You get the same lessons. But you won't all learn the same amount at the same time.

Maybe you're a late "popper" in a certain area. That doesn't mean something is wrong with you. We all learn at our own pace. With a growth mindset, you know that you are capable of learning anything you set your mind to. Believing in yourself is the first step.

CHAPTER 6

Your Mindset Matters

Amazing things can happen when you keep going and believe in yourself. With a growth mindset, you give yourself the best chance to succeed. So . . .

What do **you** want to succeed at?

Here's how to do it:

- Set a goal!
- Keep practicing.
- Celebrate when you succeed—AND when you fail. Both help you get better.
- Stay resilient when it gets tough.
- Stay positive.

You can learn tough stuff! You can do hard things! The only question is: What do you want to try next?

GLOSSARY

feedback: when someone tells you about how you perform at something, so you can get better

fixed mindset: when you believe that you can't learn something or get better at something

goal: something you aim for or try to do

growth mindset: when you believe that can learn how to do something or get better at things

mindset: your set of beliefs or attitude about what you can learn or do

progress: when you improve or get closer to completing something

resilient: when you are able to keep trying or recover from difficulty (pronounced reh-ZIL-yent)

About the Author and Illustrator

Shannon Anderson has taught in Indiana for 25 years, from first grade through college level. She was named one of ten teachers who "amazed and inspired us" by the *Today Show.* Shannon loves to write books for kids and visit schools to share the power of writing and of having a growth mindset.

Steve Mark is a freelance illustrator and a part-time puppeteer. He lives in Minnesota and is the father of three and the husband of one. Steve has illustrated many books for children, including *Ease the Tease!* and *Make a Friend, Be a Friend* from the Little Laugh & Learn™ series and all the books in the Laugh & Learn® series for older kids.

Other Great Resources from Free Spirit

Y Is for Yet
A Growth Mindset
Alphabet
by Shannon Anderson,
illustrated by Jacob Souva

For ages 4–8. 40 pp.;
HC; full-color; 8¼" x 9".

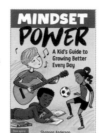

Mindset Power
A Kid's Guide to Growing
Better Every Day
by Shannon Anderson,
illustrated by Violet Lemay

For ages 9–13. 128 pp.;
PB; 2-color; 6" x 9".

Ease the Tease
by Judy S. Freedman
and Mimi P. Black,
illustrated by Steve Mark

For ages 6–9. 84 pp.;
PB; full-color; 6¼" x 8".

Make a Friend,
Be a Friend
by Eric Braun,
illustrated by Steve Mark

For ages 6–9. 88 pp.;
PB; full-color; 6¼" x 8".

How to Take the ACHE
Out of Mistakes
by Kimberly Feltes Taylor
and Eric Braun,
illustrated by Steve Mark

For ages 8–13. 128 pp.;
PB; full-color; 5⅛" x 7".

All You Can Imagine
written and illustrated by
Bernardo Marçolla

For ages 5–8. 36 pp.; HC w/
jacket; full-color; 9¼" x 10".

Interested in purchasing multiple quantities and receiving volume discounts?
Contact edsales@freespirit.com or call 1.800.735.7323 and ask for Education Sales.

Many Free Spirit authors are available for speaking engagements, workshops, and keynotes.
Contact speakers@freespirit.com or call 1.800.735.7323.

For pricing information, to place an order, or to request a free catalog, contact:

Free Spirit Publishing • 6325 Sandburg Road, Suite 100 • Minneapolis, MN 55427-3674
toll-free 800.735.7323 • local 612.338.2068 • fax 612.337.5050
help4kids@freespirit.com • freespirit.com